The Lighthouse

The Lighthouse

Inspiring Poetry for the Stormy Seasons of Life

JEFFREY JACOB KASPAR

Foreword by Jonathan Splawn

RESOURCE *Publications* · Eugene, Oregon

Resource Publications
An Imprint of Wipf and Stock Publishers
199 W. 8th Ave., Suite 3
Eugene, OR 97401

www.wipfandstock.com

PAPERBACK ISBN: 979-8-3852-2442-5
HARDCOVER ISBN: 979-8-3852-2443-2
EBOOK ISBN: 979-8-3852-2444-9

07/07/25

Unless otherwise noted, all scriptures are from the KING JAMES VERSION, public domain.

Lord be my Lighthouse,
Beacon in the night.
Illuminating a path
Away from sadness and fright.

Turn your eyes and fix your gaze
Let the light of Christ fill your eyes
See each moment as a new beginning
Each second a newly found prize.

In him was life; and the life was the light of men. And the light
shineth in darkness; and the darkness comprehended it not.

John 1:4

Contents

SECTION 2: WHEN YOU FEEL LIKE YOU'RE BROKEN

SECTION 3: HOPE AND INSPIRATION

Foreword

My name is Jonathan Splawn, I am currently Senior Pastor of Hope Church in Rhome Texas. I have worked with Accelerated Christian Education, and Cumberland Presbyterian Children's Home in past years.

My wife Holly and I have been married for over 22 years and have been blessed with 7 children. Five Natural and two Supernatural (Adopted) ranging from 4 to 21 years of age. We live on a small farm in Alvord Texas.

Meeting Jeffrey Kaspar or "Jeff" was a Divine appointment. After being led by a vision to our building, he later came to our gathering the following Sunday morning. Unlike many so called "Prophets" Jeff didn't ask for a moment or a microphone during the service. Jeff approached me privately after I had finished bringing the message to tell me something he felt the LORD had given him to tell me. As he began explaining who he was, Holy Spirit quickly qualified and confirmed his heart and this Word in my spirit.

Ever since that time, we have been brothers and fellow bondservants in Christ Jesus. Hunting, fishing, praising and praying together as the Lord gives opportunity. Jeff has been an Encouraging, Vulnerable and Authentic man of God that has helped me through difficult seasons of Discouragement, testing and trials by God's Grace flowing through Him.

My favorite poem that Jeff wrote, he brought as he spoke at Hope Church.

The title of the poem is 'In the middle' I hope and pray you find Encouragement, peace and hope in the Holy Spirit inspired pages of this book, and be blessed in the midst of whatever season you find yourself in with Jesus/Yeshua our LORD and King.

Pastor Jonathan Splawn

Acknowledgments

The greatest gift I have been given in this life is the gift God the Father gave me in His Son Jesus when He offered Him up at the Cross. Thank You Holy Spirit for drawing me to Your Son Jesus and teaching me so much about how precious and special Jesus truly is. And thank You Jesus from every part of me for loving me enough to die for me. Everything I have that's beautiful in my heart and life is from You.

I want to thank the editors and staff at Wipf and Stock Publishers, for making this book, my very first book possible to be published and distributed.

Scripture quotations from The Authorized (King James) Version. Rights in the Authorized Version in the United Kingdom are vested in the Crown. Reproduced by permission of the Crown's patentee, Cambridge University Press

With thanks also to the editors at Agape Review Online Journal where the following poems were first distributed to the public through their online journal.

The Lighthouse
How Beautiful
What Love Really Means
Rock Bottom
Love Is
In His Love
Heart Closed to All
Freedom's Song

Broken Prayers

Our Servant King

Tell Me the Story

My deepest gratitude to my family and friends for supporting me in my journey to healing from addiction and trauma. Thanks to my dad Jay Kaspar and his wife Neva Kaspar. Thanks to my brothers Jamie Kaspar and his wife Jeri Kaspar for their continued support and help. Thanks to my brother Jeremy Kaspar for helping me during some of my worst times and supporting me through my journey to getting healthy.

Special appreciation to Skip Drissel for good advice and fellowship over our 40+ year friendship. Without the help and guidance of him and his family I wouldn't be here today.

Thanks to my long time friend Shone Curole for good advice and all the long talks. We have helped each other and supported each other through some of the hardests times during our walk through this life.

Thank you to Pastor Jonathan Splawn for being a trustworthy brother in Christ and source of good advice and guidance. God led us into each other's lives and it has been a wonderful and supportive friendship.

Thank you to Steve and Betty Neese, Steve and Misti Martin, Gayle Draper-Lindemann (Ms Kitty), and many others for taking the time to read my poetry and continually encourage me on this journey.

Introduction

My sincerest hope is that my poetry helps others feel the love and adoration Christ has for us in a new and profound way. As I was choosing which poems to include from my collection, I went back to my writing journals and came across the below poem titled "Lord Be My Compass." I believe to be the first poem I wrote for the Lord during a time I was recovering from suicidal tendencies after my divorce. The title poem for the novel is called "The Lighthouse" written during a time of deep depression where the Lord kept showing me over and over His tender mercies. The love of Jesus was my beacon in the night and His love was the light that led me out of the darkness.

LORD BE MY COMPASS

JUNE 20, 2017
This was the first poem I wrote to the Lord I believe

Lord be my Compass.
Because I'm lost.
But I see a way out.
It came at a cost.
Lord be my Lighthouse,
beacon in the night.
Illuminating a path
away from sadness and fright.
Lord be my lungs,
because mine stopped breathing.
Anger has quelled,
I'm no longer seething.
Lord be my help,
my guide, be true.
Help me live my life,
All just for You.

In Jesus name.
Amen

SECTION 1

The Love of God

THE LIGHTHOUSE

*~Jesus thank You for being our beacon in the dark
guiding us home to Your arms and to safety.*

Jesus is on the throne
Joy is filling my soul
The Holy Spirit is in my heart
Reminding me God is in control

I've got breakfast in my belly
Hot coffee in my cup
Every day brings new miracles
If I'll just keep looking up

Ignore the brush fires
Distractions burning all around
Let Jesus lay them all to rest
Buried 6 feet underground

The cross reminds my heart to trust
In the Blood and in Jesus scars
At Calvary the battle won
His victory written in the stars

Every day my mind gets lost
In a foggy haze of doubt
Swimming in the voice of my past
Yet each day I hear a heavenly SHOUT

LOOK UP AND TURN YOUR EYES
CHILD LET ME HELP YOU FIX YOUR GAZE
MY BLOOD IS THE BEACON
CUTTING THROUGH THE FOGGY HAZE

My heart the unfailing lighthouse
On the majestic shores in the sky
My love for you is the light
Shining from my throne on high

Turn your eyes and fix your gaze
Focus on my love for you
My strength is steady and secure
My love will always pull you through

You've never been lost
In the foggy mists of pain
You're never gone from my sight
The Cross forever your greatest gain

Turn your eyes and fix your gaze
Let the light of Christ fill your eyes
See each moment as a new beginning
Each second a newly found prize

Each moment brings new opportunities
To plunge the depths of my love
Bringing favor wisdom blessings
Sent from my heart above.

Prayer

Heavenly Father,

Thank You for always being a steady and constant beacon of love and hope gently leading us through the darkest valleys back to Your loving arms. Thank You for always knowing how to get through to us no matter how lost we feel. I pray that these poems touch the hearts of those who read them in the same tender and loving way You touched my heart as we wrote them together. Thank You for Your Holy Spirit, my Best Friend who tells me the story of Jesus and unveils the beauty of Jesus in greater glory and detail. For anyone who is currently walking through those dark places in life, I pray Jesus that Your love be their beacon leading them to safe shores.

In Jesus name.
Amen

LOVE IS

*~ Thank You Jesus for placing Your love in our hearts
and then teaching us how to love one another.*

Love is looking deep inside
And admitting when you're wrong
Love is trusting that your life
Is held in Jesus hands so strong

All the tears you've cried
Could fill the oceans vast
And when all the crying's done
Grace makes us whole at last.

Love is learning to let go
Of the anchors and ties that bind
Love is wanting to be free
From the lies that tightly wind

Love descended from heaven on high
Love came down to give us hope
Jesus came to give us new life
Tethered forever to Grace perfect rope

Love is perfectly displayed
When You look at Jesus on the Cross
Love is the empty tomb
Without His love we'd all be lost

The scars on Jesus hands and feet
The spear that pierced His side
He bore the weight of all my sin
He died for us all with arms spread wide

Love is perfectly portrayed
In the Grace His Forgiveness brings
Love is giving up your life
So those you love will fly on eagle's wings

Jesus showed us all on that day
Exactly what love really means
That His love always finds a way
No matter how black the night may seem

His Love is free and has no conditions
No strings or hoops to jump through
His Love is patient kind and gentle
It's given freely to me and you.

Jesus Blood holds every answer
His Resurrection sealed our fate
Let down your walls let Love inside
Do it now before it's too late.

Prayer

Father,

thank You for sending Your precious Son to die for us. Thank You for showing us what Love truly is and how deep Your love runs for us. Please help us share the Love and Light of Jesus to those around us today so that they can experience Your Love and Grace as You use each of us as your hands and feet throughout this day. Put people into our lives that help grow and foster bonds and connections that are loving and supportive. Bless our families and friends with the Love and Grace of Your precious Son Father overflowing in their lives.

In Jesus name.
Amen

FATHER THANK YOU FOR JESUS.

~ Father thank You for giving us the gift of Your Son Jesus

Father Thank You for Jesus.
Thank You for the Cross.
Thank You for Your Grace.
Thank You for finding me when I'm lost.

Thank You for the whipping stone.
Where Jesus stripes healed my wounds.
Thank You for the cold and silent
Stone walls of the empty tomb.

Thank You for never letting go
When I run away and hide.
Thank You Jesus for helping me
Remember I'm alive.

Thank You Jesus for being there
When everyone else leaves.
Thank You for helping my heart
Remember to believe.

Thank You for loving me
When the world says leave me be.
Thank You Jesus for opening my heart
Thank You for helping me see.

Your Grace always finds a way.
Your Grace is what I need.
Your Grace is what lifts my spirits.
Your Grace on which I feed. .

Thank You for Your courage.
When my own heart starts to fail.
Thank You for cutting loose my anchors.
Helping me chart new seas to sail.

Thank You for looking down
From your throne with eyes ablaze.
Thank You for Your Holy Fire
Cutting through my foggy haze.

Thank You Jesus for being love.
For Your joy and peace multiplied. !
Thank You for never leaving.
For always being by my side.

Thank You for your death.
For Your suffering and Your pain.
Thank You for counting me as worthy.
For being my precious lamb who was slain

Prayer

Father,

Thank You for offering up for us all Your one and only Son Jesus on the Cross. He died to redeem us and make a way for us all to come home to Your arms in heaven some day soon. Father the precious gift of Your only Son that You offered up for us all is the most loving and beautiful gift to us all. Jesus truly is the treasure of heaven and the reason that love and light exist in this world. Father thank You for the gift of Your Son. He freely and willingly offered Himself up for us all at the Cross and proved that Your love for us Father is truly the greatest gift that could ever have been given to anyone.

In Jesus name.
Amen

VOICE OF LOVE

~ Thank You Jesus for Your Voice of Love
singing a song of hope to my heart.

I picked up my pen today
Not knowing where the words would go
What story Lord will we write together
I trust Your Spirit through me will flow

Will this be a mournful song
A story of sickness death and pain
Or will it be a siren song of hope
That turns hearts to the Cross again

While we live here on this earth
Life is a beautiful harmony containing both
The Cross gives our pains deeper meaning
The Voice of Love is now so very close

The Voice of Love is forever singing
Each note so delicate soft and pure
Yet sung with such strength and confidence
By the Blood my heart can now be sure

The Voice of Love gives us courage to get back up
When life knocks us flat on our face
His very own Spirit now lives within us
Singing to our heart a beautiful song of Jesus Grace

I hear the Voice of Love calling out my name
Saying child I've heard your tears it's ok to cry
My Voice of Love will give you strength
We'll walk each moment together so let's try

Let's try to love those around us
Let's try to be patient compassionate and kind
Let's bring help to the lost and broken
When You walk in my strength child you will find

That through the Cross even the pains have a purpose
I'll use each tear in the blueprints to rebuild your heart
Because every tear you've ever cried
I mingle it's story with Grace for a brand new start

My very Voice is the source of all Love
I sing a song to your heart written just for you
Because I knew before I formed you in secret places
That your tears one day would obscure your view

I Am the Voice of Love inside you
Singing a song that resurrects dead hopes and dreams
I sing a song to the heavens and to all creation
And through my Spirit it's melody gives you the means

To cross the greatest span of the oceans
He'll help you ascend the highest mountain
And when you find yourself in darkest valley
My Voice of Love lifts you up again and again

I've already sung your victory to the stars
Recorded the song in Blood in my book of love
My Grace and love will forever rain down on you
Carried by my Spirit as gentle as a morning dove

Prayer

Jesus,

Thank You for being the soft gentle Voice of Love forever singing into our hearts and minds; pouring Your peace and love into every broken place inside us. Thank You for knowing what we need every moment and for Your Sacrifice on the Cross to become our provider and salvation. Help us all incline our ears and our hearts towards Your wondrous voice so that Jesus Voice of Love can transform us all from the inside out.

In Jesus name.
Amen

WHAT LOVE REALLY MEANS

~Jesus teaches us how to love those around
us and how to love ourselves.

I know that I'm loved
In a way that cannot be described
That Lord Jesus came down
For me He suffered and died

He saw underneath
The stain of my life
He said child You're mine
The tomb says You'e alive

I'll love You for you
Just as you are
Child you see yourself as dirty
But You're brighter than the stars

What the world has discarded
Tossed aside and condemned
Child You are mine forever
My love will always defend

This is the way
The path I've prepared
I've already won the war for you
There's no need to be scared

I'm the Lord God Almighty
Jesus Christ your Redeemer and King
I've made my home in your heart
You're hidden under my wing

You've never been lost
I've always been right here
Please child don't close your eyes
Whisper your prayers right in my ear

I'll wrap my arms around you
In a love you cannot yet surmise
I'll heal all your broken parts
I'll wipe all the tears from your eyes

I'll love you forever
I'll show you what love really means
You'll never again be afraid
No matter how dark the night seems

The light I've placed inside you
Living waters springing forth
Because I see your true value
I know exactly what you're worth

You're a priceless treasure
A precious unique work of art
Come child you're now mine
Your home is forever my heart

These are my words
To my precious little one
From Your Father who's Glory
Shines brighter than the sun

Prayer

Jesus,

We love because You first loved us, all the way to the Cross with arms spread wide to receive us into Your arms. Because of You we have the beautiful chance to experience a love that is beyond our ability to comprehend it. Thank You for teaching us what love is and for demonstrating Love in action through Your sacrifice.

In Jesus name
Amen

IN HIS LOVE

*~Jesus thank You for the mystery and the wonder
contained within the depths of Your love for us.*

This is why we're here
To live life sharing love
Wanting hearts to overflow
Love pouring from Jesus heart above

We love because He first loved us
When He placed His love inside
Then from that seed love must be shared
With our loved ones by our side

Each moment we share together
Offers new chances to express
The love of Jesus bursting forth
From our heart inside our chest

His love heals all our wounds
His perfect love casts out all fear
Each act of kindness plants a seed
Carrying our love from far to near

At the Cross all His love poured out
In Crimson red for you and me
Then from the tomb our Lord emerged
When resurrected on day three

His love for us has no end
It's infinite perfect and complete
The free gift of His love for all
Issued from the Mercy seat

His perfect love fills every crack
Every imperfection inside our heart
His love grinds stony hearts to dust
Transforms our pain to works of art

Compared to His great love for us
Our offering to Him seems so small
Yet He counts us all as priceless treasures
His love gives us courage to stand tall

In His love what once was broken
Is remade reshaped made whole
What once was dead is given new life
Resurrection is our Savior's goal

He is the Way the Truth the Life
His love won't allow Him to forsake
His promise stands eternal
Though the entire creation should quake

In His love we're no longer broken
No longer confounded confused or lost
We're now covered with His Righteousness
Redeemed by His own blood on Calvary Cross

Prayer

Jesus,

This life is hard and it seems to get harder every day to find ways to connect with those around us in meaningful ways that impact lives. But that's why we're here, to live this life day by day, moment by moment, sharing our lives together in love. Your love within us Jesus grows and multiplies to the point it feels like our hearts will explode, so we need opportunities to connect with others so that we can share that love with them and lift each other up. Please help us find ways to connect in deeper more meaningful ways.

In Your precious name
Amen

HOW BEAUTIFUL

*~I'm filled with awe and wonder at how
beautiful Your ways are Lord*

How beautiful are the ways of God
So much higher than I can comprehend
My mind is frozen in awe and wonder
At the Love and Grace the Cross did send

The hearts of stone will be turned
To fertile soil to receive good seed
Your Son has prepared for us a harvest
Your Blood has covered for our every need

Soon we'll meet Jesus in the clouds
Transformed in the twinkling of an eye
And when we hear the trumpet sound
On eagles wings we all will fly

To our new mansions of gold
To beauty our mind cannot comprehend
We'll walk forever with Jesus hand in hand
Safe in the arms of our Lord and friend

He will wipe away every single tear
In His presence only love and grace
And when He fixes His gaze upon you
There's only loving kindness on His face

He died on the Cross just for you
His Resurrection declared you're free
He sent His own Spirit to live inside us
He's returning soon so come and see

Lord Jesus we can't wait to see You
Please come quick and take us home
Fill our hearts with love unimaginable
On streets of gold we'll forever roam

Prayer

Father,

Thank You for being so much more than we can possibly comprehend. Your ways are beautiful and lovely and as we walk this life and see Your purpose and plan unfold day by day around us, it leaves us more awestruck at who You are and what You did for us at the Cross. We are in awe of You Jesus. Thank You.

In Jesus name
Amen

LET IT RAIN

*~Lord let Your Love and Grace rain down
on us this day and make us whole.*

Each morning we wake up
And consider the day ahead
We wonder how we'll get through the storm
We pray not to stumble and just be lead

We pray that through each situation
Which has it's very own troubles and worries
We be filled with revelation like dew from heaven
So that we are not shaken through life's hurries

Let Your Spirit fall like rain upon us
Fill us in our heart and mind
Let peace reign within our spirit
So that the pains and hurts just fall behind

Your love and Grace are a torrential flood
Pouring down and filling us on the inside
Becoming a river carrying us towards Your throne
A storm of love so great no need to hide

You promise Your goodness and mercy rain down
On the just and unjust all the same
At the Cross Your Son gave His life
He died for us all that's why He came

Let it rain down bringing revelation
Let it rain blessings from Your throne on high
Let it rain down to all Your children
Let it rain to remind us redemption draws nigh

Let it rain down healing straight from Jesus
Let it rain down hope and help abroad
Let it rain down Grace and wisdom
Let it rain down we pray Lord just because

Just because Jesus died for us
He gave it all up for us at the Cross
Then on Day 3 He rose from earth and stone
Let it rain to remind us how great the cost

Father You gave us Your very best
The most precious treasure in all Creation
Through Jesus we have forgiveness
Sanctified and sealed by Your Son's Resurrection

We're now Justified and made Righteous
Your Spirit is our very best friend
So Lord let it rain down on us all
From the Cross resurrection life reigns within

He is the rain gently falling around us
The dew from heaven that restores our soul
He brought a tidal wave of Grace to lift us up
Grace is the rain that heals us and makes us whole

Prayer

Heavenly Father,

Every day in this place filled with sin is a struggle in some way for us all. We need Your Love and Grace to lift us up and carry us through the moments of each day. Without You leading us and guiding our steps we will surely fail and fall. But that's why You came Jesus, You died on the Cross so that today You can gently rain down Your blessings into our lives to give us hope and help. Please let the dew of heaven rain down on us all and lead us ever towards Your heart.

In Jesus name
Amen

OH THE GRACE

Where will this walk take me
Is there a point to this
We wake-up and walk alone
Never knowing a loving kiss

Hurt by those who say they love us
Betrayed through promises broken
Lies dripping off everyone's tongue
Venom flying with every word spoken

But everywhere you look
When you stare deep in their eyes
You see they're wearing masks
Hiding their pain behind a clever disguise

If only they had the courage
To let down their walls and stand
Let Jesus in their heart to reign
Bring joy to their life again

He binds up wounds meant to destroy
He heals deep hurts and lacerations
Brings joy where once was darkness
He makes us His new creation

He IS He WAS He ALWAYS WILL BE
He died for us He set us free
The Cross the Blood our guarantee
His light His love makes demons flee

I once cowered in fear
Shame and shadow my disguise
Then Love tore down my walls
I stared directly into my Savior's eyes

No judgement blame or guilt
No anger or wrath upon His face
Only love acceptance and joy
Mercy Truth and Grace

The Grace that ripped wide the grave
The Grace that destroyed sin's power
The Grace that opened heaven's Gates
The Grace that makes death cower

The Grace that could see through
The life of suffering and pain I'd wrought
The Grace that saw me as worthy
With His own Blood I've now been bought

Oh the Grace that captured me
Oh the Grace that cured my wounds
Oh the Grace that set me free
The Grace that saved me from my tomb

Father help me see through fresh eyes
The life and love of my King
Help me learn all about His life
Help me worship dance and sing.

This is why I get up each day
Why I can now rest easy late at night
Because Jesus saw me as priceless
Worthy and beautiful in His sight

Prayer

Jesus

The hurts and pains we carry gives us scars and leave wounds nobody can physically see with their eyes. Wounds in our very soul and the very fabric of our being. So we wear masks and pretend we're not hurt and broken, hiding our real selves behind fake smiles and half-hearted laughter. Holy Spirit teach us each day about the Grace that pours from the Cross and of all the benefits the Grace of Jesus gives us today. It's Grace that gives Jesus access to all those secret rooms in our heart where those wounds lie and it's Grace that heals us and makes us whole. Please let Your Grace teach us and guide us to wholeness and health and into Your arms.

In Jesus name
Amen

THE PROMISE

~ Thank You Jesus that Your promises cannot be undone.

There is a promise spoken
One that cannot be undone
It's written into all creation
From the heart of God's own Son

It's a promise that's so complex
In words alone it cannot be told
So it's etched in Blood and in Stone
And speaks of a love we cannot behold

He took off His Crown of Glory
Set aside His Robe of Majesty
He chose to come and save us
He chose to die for you and me

He said I love You exactly as You are
Let my love be Your guiding light
My gentle Grace will heal all your hurts
I'll teach you to walk by faith not sight

Your heart is what I treasure most
I promise to never leave your side
I'll place my own Spirit within you
To be Your Helper Friend and Guide

I suffered on the Cross just for you
Hell and death now have no claim
Every sin across your whole life
Is forgiven when you believe in my name

I promise that I am coming soon
To carry you away with me
We'll walk along my heavenly shores
I'm Lord and King so come and see

Come and see my empty tomb
Lay down your hurts and pains
I'll wrap my arms 'round you
All is healed by my blood stains

I promise Child you are enough
And all those hurts you try to hide
Will all be healed by my Grace
If you'll just rest in me and abide

Prayer

Father,

Thank You for the promise sealed in the Blood of Your only Son that You will love us forever if we'll only believe in Your Son. Your promise to love us exactly as we are and Your promise that You will never ever leave us even unto the end of the age. Please help us see Jesus and Your Word as the only promises that can never be broken because You are unchanging and from everlasting to everlasting. Your love for us will remain forever even unto the end of the age.

In Jesus name
Amen

SECTION 2:

When You Feel Like You're Broken

HEART OF GOD

~ Thank You Father for offering up Your very own
Heart, Your only Son, Jesus, for us at the Cross

Jesus stood in the temple
He took the scroll began to read
Today this scripture is fulfilled
The Word of God became the Seed

The Seed that changed everything
The Word of God tabernacles with men
God Immanuel means God among us
The very Heart of God yes He did descend

Jesus Himself declared His mission
To come bind up the broken hearted
Yet at the Cross His own heart was crushed
He cried out FINISHED when His Spirit departed

Blood and Water poured from the wound
When the soldier's spear pierced His side
Our Saviors heart had been cut in twain
He died for me with arms spread wide

My heart's been broken into a thousand pieces
Yet my Jesus knows exactly how to repair
Repair it more beautiful than it was before
His Love and Grace destroy despair

The hands that hold all creation
The hands that formed beauty from the void
Are the same nail pierced hands that heal
The broken hearts the world destroyed

He died from a broken heart
So that you and I can have ours healed
The Love of God was on display for all
The Heart of God has been revealed

Prayer

Father.

The gift You gave the world when You offered up Your only Son for us on the Cross, He is beautiful beyond compare. Jesus is Your very own heart Father and inside of it is the most beautiful love imaginable. Thank You for revealing Your heart, Your love poured out as Your Son sacrificed Himself to redeem us back to Your arms. He died so that we can come home to You and be with You forever. Thank You for Your sacrifice.

In Jesus name
Amen

PAPER MAN

~ Thank You Jesus for writing Your Word,
Your story, onto the pages of my life.

I'm a paper man living a paper life
Easily crumbled up and tossed aside
Nothing to give the paper structure
All I can do is trust Jesus and abide

A paper life that's easily forgotten
Barely a memory to this world
Trying to find my role and purpose
Through the tribulations that unfurled

Paper is such a simple thing
By itself it holds no weight
Then the Word of life took His pen
Wrote a story of love to erase the hate

Paper by itself is common
But when it's filled with the Word
The message gives the paper strength
From the voice of love that's heard

Jesus loves to take common things
To confound the minds of the strong
He takes those the world discarded
Says child you're mine to Me you belong

I'll write a beautiful story on your pages
I'll fill the lines with joy and hope anew
My Word is a solid foundation
My Spirit will always lead you through

When the Word is mingled in the story
Hope eternal bursts forth from Love
Paper and Word become incorruptible
Anchored to Jesus heart above

Jesus thank You for writing a new story
Inked in Blood then stone at the tomb
Thank You for being my anchor of hope
Inside Your heart is my special room

Prayer

Lord,

There have been times in my life that I felt like I was hollow and made of paper. No substance or firmness or solidity to me. Easily crumpled up and tossed aside by those I thought cared about me. The wonderful thing about paper though is that by itself it has no weight, but when the right words are penned and written on its surface, the paper which once was weightless and common suddenly becomes heavy and powerful through the message written upon its lines. Thank You Jesus for writing Your message, Your story, Your Word spoken over my life onto the pages of my life wrapped around this hollow earthen vessel. Now because of You, Your Blood, because of the Cross, I am no longer empty and hollow, I am filled with Your love and Grace and You've given me a purpose and story. You give my life value and make every hurt and tear worth the journey. I am a priceless treasure because You chose to love me and wrote Yoru story only the pages of my life. Thank You for the beautifully written story. I can't wait to walk out the next chapter with You.

In Jesus name
Amen

HEART CLOSED TO ALL

~ Thank You Jesus for finding us when we hide

All the fear and worry
You store down deep inside
Pains that hurt your heart so much
The real you ran away to hide

You walk this life with eyes open
But your heart is closed to all
You put on paper masks with smiles
Inside you hide behind prison walls

I see you hiding in the dark
Scared to ever try again
You believe you're forgotten
Without a single loving friend

But I hear every tear you cry
Even the silent ones you keep hidden
Behind locked doors inside your heart
Marked Keep Out Entry Forbidden

My Beloved I've come to find you
My Grace and Love will heal your pain
I died on the Cross just for this day
Just whisper in the dark my name

You're not broken not useless
Not a complete waste of space
I'm the Lord God Jesus Christ
I'm bringing all my Love and Grace

All your mistakes and failures
They matter not to me
To me You're still my sweet child
I'm right here just come and see

I've forgiven everything already
At the Cross You'll find Redemption
There's nothing inside those rooms
My Love can't heal with great perfection

In my heart You're already accepted
I love You exactly as you are right now
You're my sweet lost sheep I've come to find
We'll walk this life together I'll show you how

My strength will give your feet new steps
My wings will carry you on new winds
Come child let me wipe those tears
It's time that our new journey begins.

Prayer

Father,

As we go through the struggles of this life we get hurt and when we do we tend to close our hearts off from the world. Retreat into ourselves. Feeling unloved. Unwanted. Undervalued. We put up walls and barriers to keep everyone out. To protect ourselves and keep anyone from ever hurting us again. Because if we don't let them in, they can't hurt us. Please help find a way for us to remember that You're right here in our heart with us. And that to You, we matter. Our hurts and pains matter to You and You cry every tear alongside with us when we're hurting. Give us the courage to let down the walls and try again in life. Try again to love. Try again to laugh. Try again to leave the hurts in the past for good.

In Jesus name
Amen

BROKEN PRAYERS

~ When we pray from a place inside so hurt that even our prayers feel broken because we can't find the right words to speak to You

If i just keep my prayers positive
Force a smile onto my face
Say pretty words that sound good
Pretend I'm not in that broken place

Never let anyone see my pain
Not even my Father up in Heaven
Then the sadness buried deep
Won't pollute my heart like leaven

A gentle voice inside me whispers
Its ok to let Me see Your pain
I suffered on the Cross just for you
Child let My pain become your gain

Im not afraid of all that hurt
Inside those forgotten rooms
I'll sit and wait until you're ready
To come meet me at the tomb

Come and see my resting place
Bury it with me under stone
I've already shattered every chain
Prepared your place beside my throne

I prefer honesty spoken from way down deep
Even if the words come out broken
Child let's about those deep hurts
Instead of empty flowery words spoken

Its your heart child that I seek most
Your heart is my most prized treasure
The payment i gave for it at the Cross
Was priceless beyond measure.

Prayer

Father,

There are times in our lives that the pain is too deep, the emotion too overwhelming that we don't have the words to express the sadness, sorrow, and hurt that we're feeling. We try to talk about it with family friends and in prayer but the right words are lost to us. Unintelligible words pour out of our mouth while crying rivers of tears. The hurt so deep that even our prayers for help sound broken. Since we're broken and our prayers are broken, we begin to believe that not even God could possibly love me at a time like this. How could He love someone so lost. But You prefer that kind of honesty, pouring out our hearts casting our cares on You because You care for us and You are touched by our infirmities and cry every tear with us. You prefer sobbing outpourings from the heart over flowery words that skirt around the real problems within us. Words that sound good and flow together like a song but have no heart or depth, leaving those deep hurts in our hearts where they fester and hurt us even more. Please help heal the hurts inside, give us a way to open up and talk to You about them so that we can invite You into that place of pain to heal us.

In Jesus name
Amen

ROCK BOTTOM

~Rock bottom becomes your firm foundation in Jesus

The bottom rushes towards your face
Faster than you believed it could
You keep falling over and over
Something you never believed you would

Yet the thought of starting over
Doesn't sting like it used to
The rocky bottom that awaits
Offers security to help you through

You now find peace and comfort
In that place that once caused fear
Because standing there on the Rock
You remember Lord Jesus is near

He promised to never leave your side
He walks beside you every single day
He will lift you out of that rocky place
He is the Life the Truth the Way

The winds can howl, Flood waters rise
Thunder shakes, Lightning splits the skies
The lion can roar, Let the enemy despise
This storm is not your end, nor your demise

Because the Rock is your steady ground
On His name you built your foundation
He died to meet you in that place
To be your Redeemer, Restorer, Salvation

Because He himself descended down
At the tomb He Himself hit rock bottom
Sealed in that stone He took up His Crown
He declared your name you're not forgotten

Formed by love in His own hands
You are His precious child
Your home is not here on this earth
You're not lost wandering in the wild

The middle of His heart is your true home
By His Blood alone you've been freed
The Tomb was where He Himself hit rock bottom
Where He declared Child you're free indeed

Prayer

Father,

There are times in our lives when we just seem to keep on endlessly falling into empty space. No sure footing to stand on and nothing to hold onto. All the world around us moves like shifting sand. At some point we hit rock bottom and find ourselves in a pit so deep we have no idea what to do, where we are, where we're going, and sometimes rock bottom is so far underground that we even forget who we are. Standing there at rock bottom, all we can do is look up and that's where we find Jesus waiting for us. He's been patiently waiting for us to come to the end of ourselves so that rock bottom, bedrock, the Rock of Jesus can be the sure foundation He will rebuild our lives upon. Jesus thank You for being the solid foundation of our lives that withstand any storm and hold back every flood giving us stability, safety, and security in Your loving arms covered by Grace.

In Jesus name
Amen

OUR SERVANT KING

~ Thank You Father for sending us Your Son to be our Redeemer and Lord and Savior. A Servant King that none can compare to.

He is tender hearted
Soft gentle and kind
He's promised He'll save
He'll leave none behind

He treads softly
Through hearts that are broken
Bringing love and Grace
Through His every word spoken

He binds up the feeble
He rescues the weak
Those who think they're forgotten
Yes it's them that He seeks

A bruised reed
He will never break
He brings resurrection
He'll do whatever it takes

Smoking Flax won't be quenched
Their flame never snuffed out
He placed them in Father's hands
Restoration is what He's about

When their love towards God
Is ready to expire
He rekindles their flame
With Grace to fuel their fire

Their wick is renewed
Burns brightly again
Cause Jesus treads softly
Through hearts of men

Girdled with love
To wash our feet
Teach us we're whole
In Him we're complete

We're not broken not lost
Because in Him we're found
Free from the chains and barbed wire
That chokes hearts tightly wound

He'll never leave those
Who cry desperate tears
He comes to those hurting
He shatters their fears

He's a Servant King set apart
There's none quite like Jesus
He'll let nothing separate
He'll remove what's between us

His love is surmounting
His Grace superabounding
His heart overflowing
His Glory shining and glowing

His Spirit descending
To hearts that need mending
The Seconds I'm counting
On Eagle's wings we'll be mounting

The downtrodden belong to Jesus
They are forever His pride
They'll inherit His kingdom
They'll sit on thrones by His side.

Prayer

Father,

There has never been nor will there ever be anyone like Your Son Jesus. There is no other love that compares to His. There is no other glory or beauty that compares with who He is and what He did for us at the Cross. Yet He didn't come to be served as royalty, He came to serve those He loves. He said whoever among you is greatest will be the least in heaven. His majesty and throne are above all yet He came down to wash our feet, to live a life serving those He came to die for. Thank You Jesus for teaching us what it means to let love lead and guide us. Please help us model Your leadership as we serve those around us that we love. Help us be humble and wash the feet of the people in our lives we care for.

In Jesus name
Amen

CHRIST IN ME

~ Thank You Jesus for making me a new
creation full of Your love and Grace.

The race has already been won
The prize has already been given
The most valuable treasure in all creation
Is the truth that in Christ I've been forgiven

I gave my heart to my king
As a young teenager full of pride
The Holy Spirit drew my heart to Jesus
And at the Altar He came to dwell inside

In that moment I was transformed
In an instant I was made new
Your Grace and love filled my heart
But I didn't understand what next to do

So I ran fromr Your face for years
Got lost in the loneliest desolate places
People passed in and out of my life
Looking back it's just a blur of faces

At Rock bottom was where I found
That I have never walked alone
Jesus was waiting there for me
To lift me up and carry me home

No matter how far I ran
No matter how hard I tried
He never ever let go of me
He was always right there by my side

He began the process of rebuilding my heart
Making it more beautiful than it was before
He taught me that I'm not lost or broken
That in His name by Grace He made me much more

The roads where I had been travelling
Were built on sand and paved with lies
But the Truth and freedom in His sweet name
Taught me my heart is made to soar blue skies

The old Jeff died long ago
He was crucified with Christ on a lonely tree
He made me into a new creation
Now in Him I live life more abundantly

He taught me what love truly is
He taught me who I am to Him
Now I can't help but praise His name
And do my best to share His love with friends

His Spirit teaches me fresh each day
About the love and Grace freely given to me
When I look back I see how far He's brought me
Now in the mirror I love the reflection I see

I'm being transformed from Glory to Glory
Into the image of Christ my King
My heart is crushed every time I see Him
Then reborn in the love and Grace He brings

When I look deep into my eyes reflection
I see a man full of hope who's been set free
I see a future full of possibilities in Jesus
I see the work of Christ in me

Prayer

Father,

When I look back and remember the life we've walked together, where we've been, who I used to be, then compare with today the changes are truly a wonderful work of Grace in my life. But that's the beauty of the Cross; the beauty of having the Comforter, the Holy Spirit of God living with us, helping transform us. The Cross gives us access to the love and Grace we so desperately need so that we can bear fruit unto God and not bear fruit unto death. YOur Spirit transforms us from the inside out teaching us who we are to You, and who Jesus You are to us. What You did for us, all about Your beauty and the wonders wrapped up in the Cross and the empty tomb. I pray that You help us all share the love Christ placed within us with those around us. Help us be compassionate, kind, loving, and forgiving even when others haven't earned it and don't deserve it. Give us the courage to reach out to others in need and through it, we pray that they see Christ in us and the light of Christ and His Glory be magnified.

In Jesus name
Amen

PRETENDING

~ Thank You Jesus for loving me exactly as I am.

Pretending that I am holding it all together
Pretending that everything's all ok
Pretending that I'm no longer struggling
Pretending that it's perfect every day

We get crushed from the weight
Of expectations we place on ourselves
All that pretending suffocates us
What we need is a break from our self

Take a break from all that pretending
Breathe in and out, slowly exhale
I'll let Jesus hold my heart so tender
I'll Let His soft whispers fill my sail

His arms so strong they hold all creation
Galaxies and stars dance around His feet
He sings and they dance in perfect harmony
He is strong and able to lift me out of defeat

In His arms I don't have to pretend
It's the only place I truly feel secure
He whispers words of love and kindness
He sings you're my child, Yes I'm sure

I will never let you out of my sight
I will love you forever child you're mine
Together we'll dance among the stars
I'll sing my love into your heart and mind

I died so that you don't have to pretend
I'll heal every hurt. Wipe away every tear
Here wrapped up in my arms
There's nothing you need to fear

You're torn about the path ahead
You're afraid You're not enough
But you're my child and I've already won
I've filled your heart with all the right stuff

You're a conqueror in my name
Your victory's already written in stone
I rose to declare to all creation
You are mine and my heart's your home.

Prayer

Father,

Thank You for knowing us in the most intimate ways so that we have no need to fear or hide away from You. You know us and love us exactly as we are. We have no need to pretend to be someone or something that we're not. We just trust that Your love for us has made a way through this life and that Your Spirit will lead us and guide us and help change us and transform us from glory to glory into the image of Christ. You take what we have, and You make us better, You make us complete. Your Grace completes us in ways that we didn't know we were broken. Heals hurts in our heart and soul that we forgot were in there and have just been limping along our entire lives within us. Thank You for the Cross where You died to set us free, free from ourselves and free from the wrong expectations the world and others place upon us.

In Jesus name
Amen

A HUG

~For those times words fail, a hug is the answer.

Sometimes there are no words
That can be spoken to soothe your soul
Not even words of love and support
Can heal the hurt and make you whole

When there are just no words
And every sentence and syllable fails
A hug from the arms of a loving friend
Can be the wind to fill your sail

When words fall short to ease the pain
When flowery words fail to impart
A loving touch can cure secret wounds
A hug wipes tears away from your heart

A hug itself is it's very own language
A simple hug can speak great volumes
The love wrapped up in a warm embrace
Unlocks doors in our heart to secret rooms

Those hurts in our heart we keep hidden
Locked up tight from every prying eye
All that hurt instantly feels better
Drained in an embrace with a loving sigh

A hug can silence those inner voices
A hug can bring peace amidst the storm
A hug reminds us we're not alone
A hug can calm fears in every form

At the Cross we see Jesus waiting
His Blood stained hands spread wide
His loving embrace awaits us all
Let's rest in His arms and just abide

He's strong and steady in times of trouble
His arms will hold you safe and secure
His Love and Grace will always find You
That's His promise so we can all be sure

When You feel lost abused and broken
Fall into the only arms that can save
There's no place His Hands can't reach
Not even death, hell or the grave

His love will always find You
His arms are strong to bear the weight
Let His Blood stained hands wrap 'round you
And feel His hug straight from heaven's gate.

Prayer

Father,

In those moments when words fail us and there is nothing that can be said to ease our hurt or calm our fears, a loving embrace from a friend can speak to our hearts in ways that words cannot. Thank You Jesus for giving us our emotions and for walking this life with us helping us navigate the inner turmoil that they can create within us. Thank You for giving us such beautiful ways our hearts can communicate with another's heart that transcend words alone. I pray that when we are overwhelmed and life is crashing down around us, You place into the heart of those we love to reach out and hold us close. Tell us we're going to be ok. Remind us of what You've done for us on the Cross and that in Your name, we already have the victory and have already received the most precious gift in all creation. You.

In Jesus name
Amen

LOST AND FOUND

*~Jesus thank You for not forgetting about
us in the Lost and Found*

Lord we all think we've been forgotten
Tossed into an old box in the lost and found
Abandoned with the things nobody wants
Feeling helpless and alone here on the ground

We all just want to know who we are
To know that we've never been truly lost
That someone somewhere out there loves us
We need help remembering Jesus on the Cross

He paid for us all with His precious Blood
He died so that one day our hearts can know
That to Lord Jesus we can never be lost
His heart is the fertile ground in which we grow

I hear Your voice Jesus telling me
I'm not a mistake and my life isn't all wrong
There's beauty and love amidst the pain
Grace transformed my life into a beautiful song

When I look in the mirror it's hard to remember
Your love for me is beyond what I could ever realize
That by Grace through Faith I've been redeemed
And by the Blood I'm now Your Beloved prize

Thank You Jesus for not leaving me in that box
Thank You for finding me when my memory fails
When I feel scared and wandering in the dark
You remind me that Grace has tipped the scales

The payment You made to purchase my heart
To redeem me from the Lost and Found abyss
Was worth more than all the treasure in heaven
And You sealed the contract with Grace's Kiss

Prayer

Father,

We suffer at the hands of rejection all throughout this life including when we're born. We're born rejected by our creator because of the original sin from Adam we're born with. Some of us end up feeling forgotten and lost, rejected by the ones in our lives who said they would love us unconditionally and never leave us, then did. We need help remembering that we are loved, that we are cherished, that we are valued and not abandoned or unworthy. Christ You came to redeem us and reverse the curse and now through His death and resurrection we have the honor and blessing of being sons of God and co-heirs with Him. Now through Jesus we have a home in heaven, we have a Father in heaven who loves us and cherishes us. We are part of Your eternal family Jesus and we are so thankful that we will never have to spend another lonely night forgotten in the Lost and Found.

In Jesus name
Amen

THE ONE

~Jesus thank You for being the One who holds forever.

The One who holds forever
Holds my heart in the palm of His hand
The One who promises to love me forever
Is the one in whose strength I stand

The One who conquered death and the Grave
Is the One who died on the Cross for all
The One who healed all who came
Is the One who saved us from the fall

Thank You Jesus for being the only One
The only One who can truly judge our hearts
The all-together lovely and beautiful Son of God
Is coming soon so it's time for us to start

Start Loving those all around that we see
To the left and to the right
Holding hands with those around us
Carrying each other through the darkest night

The One who persevered and conquered death
Is the one who died on that cursed tree
The One who holds my hand today
He tells me He loves me child you're free

I love the One who holds my heart
I love those around me the best I can
I hope that I make Him proud
After all He is the great I AM

Thank You Jesus for being the One
Thank You Father for sending Him down
Thank You Holy Spirit for being with me
And making sure one day I receive my crown

Thank You Father for sending Your only Son
Thank You Jesus for Your suffering
Thank You Holy Spirit for smiling down
On a lonely wretch like me

Prayer

Heavenly Father,

Thank You for sending Your only Son Jesus to come down and give us the gift of His own life poured out for me and for us all at the Cross. It is truly the most loving and beautiful thing that has ever been done in all creation. He willingly came down and sacrificed His life to redeem me from the hurts and pains the sins of my life caused within me. Thank You for freely offering up Your only Son for us all so that we have the opportunity to experience Your love for us freely through the Blood of Your only Son. The Love and Grace wrapped up in that gift can never be measured, quantified or even contemplated. It's too perfect and too beautiful and too immense to comprehend. Thank You Father for the gift of Your Son. Thank You Jesus for the gift of Your sacrifice. Thank You Holy Spirit for coming to live inside us to lead us and guide us through this life and for teaching us every day a little more about what Your precious Son died to give us.

In the name of Jesus, the most beautiful and precious and holy name ever spoken.

Amen

SECTION 3:

Hope and Inspiration

TELL ME THE STORY

~A poem written to the Holy Spirit

Holy Spirit tell me the story of Jesus
I want to hear every single word
Now don't leave out a single thing
Because each time that I have heard

The tale of love intricately woven
From Father's heart to earth
Life renews inside dead places
Resurrection bursting forth

Tell me the story of Jesus
How He healed all who came
He bound up the broken hearted
Helped those walk who once were lame

A bruised reed will not be broken
Each too precious to throw aside
Smoking flax will not be snuffed out
He counts each one as His new bride

Please tell me the story of Jesus
Of His suffering even of His death
How at the Cross He bowed His head
Dismissed His Spirit with His last breath

How the Cross reminds my heart to trust
How the tomb reminds me I once died
He carried my sins far away
Now I sit on a throne by His side

Please tell me again the story of Jesus
I need to hear every single word
I'll listen a thousand times a thousand again
It matters not how many times I've heard

The story of love written
In the fleshy tables of my heart
Jesus death and resurrection
His promise He will never ever part

Tell me the story of Jesus
Can I tell you of how He changed my life
I once was lost but in Him I'm found
He bore the burden of all my strife

My eyes which once saw only darkness
Fear consumed my every thought
Now His light chases away my shadows
Because with His Blood I was bought

Prayer

Father,

Every day has it's own struggles and worries and our mind and thoughts get lost trying to just get through each moment. We need Your Spirit each and every day to tell us the story of Jesus over and over again. Remind us of what Jesus did for us at the Cross. How He suffered and died so that each day even in the midst of our daily turmoils, we're never ever alone. He's always right there with us in the middle of each moment of each and every day. Please help our hearts remember all the wonderful benefits His sacrifice bought and sealed for us on that day long before we were born. Please help us see the Cross every day with fresh eyes and teach us new things about how much He loves us. Give us fresh oil and revelation daily to keep our hearts centered on Him and what He's done and off of ourselves and the problems we face. We love You Jesus. Holy Spirit tell us the story of Jesus.

In Jesus name
Amen

I SEE AN EMPTY GRAVE

~ When I think of Jesus I see an empty
tomb that brings peace to my heart.

Father I see an empty grave
Both ahead of me and behind
A cold stone tomb meant to destroy
Yet brings me such peace of mind

At the Cross my Savior died
The cold stone tomb that sealed my fate
In Him I was reborn in Righteousness
Now wide before me is heaven's gate

The tomb behind me is forever empty
Jesus death and Resurrection redeemed my life
The tomb reminds me with Him I died
That He bore the pain of all my strife

Father I see an empty grave
That cold stone tomb tells me I'm Yours
I'll never have to fear my fate
You've already opened up heaven's doors

The gift You sent from Your own heart
The gift containing all Your love
The gift of Jesus who laid down his life
The tomb secured my place above

The gift that makes me Righteous
The gift that fills love inside heart
The gift of the empty tomb's promise
That you'll never forsake nor part

The tomb reminds me His love for me
Has made a way to break down my walls
That I'm fearfully and wonderfully made
I can roam freely through heaven's halls

That is my home and rightful place
Paid for by my Savior's death
When His body hung on that Cross
Dismissed His Spirit with His last breath

Oh how I love that empty tomb
Now sin and death shrink back and cower
Because Jesus rose for my Justification
He returned in Glory to heaven's tower

Prayer

Father,

When I consider the Cross where Jesus bled and died for me, I see my sins laid upon Him. I see my sicknesses and diseases, my hurts and my pains, in each and every mar, mark, and stripe upon His body. He died to take them all for me so that I can have his healing life today. But my mind wants to linger there with Him hanging on that tree. Help me Father rejoince in the Cross by remembering the empty tomb where the promises that were sealed by HIs blood were then etched in stone. Jesus isn't still hanging on that tree HE IS RISEN and IS ALIVE TODAY. Help me see myself that way also. Yes I died on that Cross with Him but I also rose with Him, first in Spirit but one day I will also receive my perfected body and rise up and meet Him in the clouds. He is Risen so I am Risen and I am seated with Christ in heavenly places by Faith. Help me see myself there Father remembering that Christ didn't just die for me, HE ROSE FOR ME CONQUERING DEATH.

In Jesus name
Amen

FREEDOM'S SONG

*~ The song of Love and Grace Jesus sings to our hearts
breaks every chain and frees us from every bondage.*

The devil flings fiery darts
From hidden secret places
Meant to impale
Blood running down our faces

But each fiery arrow
Is quenched by a melody
Because my weapon is the song
Jesus sang just for me

There once was a time
I was lost in oceans of pain
Enjoying the lusts of the world
Indulging time and time again

Then I heard a melody
Piercing through the night
The most beautiful singing
Calling me into the light

It was my Beautiful Savior's voice
A song only I could hear
Telling me it's ok child
Follow my voice come near

It lulled my heart
I was instantly hypnotized
I followed it's beauty
Til I looked in Jesus eyes

The Grace in that tune
The light in His gaze
Cut through the confusion
Led me out of the foggy haze

He sang me to freedom
Songs of forgiveness and Grace
Love dripping from every note
Like honey running down my face

He sang me to wholeness
He taught me in Him I'm complete
He showed me Father's wrath
Forever covered by the Mercy seat

All Father's anger towards me
Poured into Jesus on the Cross
Now I'm redeemed and free
In His great love I am lost

Then Jesus taught me the tune
We now sing in perfect harmony
Together we sang away my pain
I'm His forever and now I'm free

Prayer

Heavenly Father,

We get caught and trapped each and every day by our own thoughts and words, believing lies. Wrong ideas about who we are to ourselves, who we are to You, who You are to us. It feels like some days the chains around our hearts are so tight we can barely believe our heart can beat and keep moving blood throughout our veins. What we need is to pause, take a moment to remember that we are not helpless victims caught in the traps sin lures us into. No we have You Jesus. We have the safety and security that the Cross and Your Spilled blood offers us. We have Your beautiful voice singing to us to freedom each and every day. Reminding us that those chains aren't holding us anymore, we've been freed by the Love and Grace still flowing endlessly from the Cross. He whom You set free Jesus is free indeed and we are free indeed. Thank You for singing to our hearts and minds the beautiful Freedom Song that causes our spirit to lift up and want to fly within us.

In Jesus name
Amen

LIFE'S SONG

*~ Thank You Jesus for giving us the beautiful melody
of Grace for us to sing and dance through this life.*

Life's song is a melody nobody can hear
It's rhythm is metered out as we move our feet
It's a beautiful combination of Grace and Love
Poured into our lives from Jesus Mercy Seat

We take the song He sings into our heart
Then dance through the moments of each day
He gives us opportunities to express and share love
If we'll just take the time to dance and play

We all walk through this life hiding
Afraid to let go and experience His love
The hurts and pains stored up inside
Are only healed by His Love from above

He understands the hurts and pains we feel
He cries with us when our hearts get broken
He came down to bind up the broken hearted
Love without action is an empty word spoken

He Himself stepped into this broken world
Then He Himself was poured out for us on the Cross
God's Divine Expression of Love went in motion
God took action to redeem all of what was lost

When you look at your neighbor's face
When you gaze into a coworkers eyes
Take the time to enjoy the moment
What you'll find might be the best surprise

Sometimes we don't need any advice
Or someone to explain all the ways we're wrong
What we need is just a few loving moments
To share our time together singing this life's song

Prayer

Father,

When we wake up each day and consider all the things we have to accomplish in this busy hectic life. We get caught up checking off items on To-Do Lists and forget that life is about much more than tasks, it's all about love. Loving those around us and those we encounter so that we can help bear each others' burdens. We love because You first loved us Jesus so now that You've placed Your love within us, we have the beautiful opportunity to share that love with those around us. This life is a song of love with Your Grace giving us the harmony and beat. Help us sing this life's song with a joyful heart and Your love overflowing into the lives of those You place in our path each day Lord.

In Jesus name
Amen

RHYTHM OF GRACE

~Everything in all creation moves to the rhythm of Grace

Everything in all creation
Sings its own unique song
That lifts up to heaven's throne
Declaring to whom it belongs

It's a song of praise and worship
To Jesus Christ our King
If we refuse to worship Him
Even the rocks will sing

The sounds of everything combine
Into a beautiful symphony of praise
A concert with a specific purpose
Declaring that Lord Jesus saves

Jesus heartbeat is the rhythm
That controls the melodious sound
The endless Grace from His heart
Matches the rhythm descending down

His Love and His Will flow freely
Perfectly matched to the rhythm of Grace
Living Water bursting from the Rock
His heartbeat keeps symphony's pace

Lord Jesus sings a song to the melody
Every note carries His Perfect love
Mending every hurting heart
He's kind and gentle as a morning dove

The song that Jesus sang to me
When I was lost scared and so alone
Mesmerized my heart and mind
His gentle voice sweetly calling me home

Come home my love to my heart
To a secret place that I've prepared
My love will light the way for you
No more darkness so you won't be scared

If your feet have no more strength
Child just rest in me and abide
I'm strong and my yoke is easy
I'll carry you forever right by my side

I'll sing to you every step
Songs declaring my Grace and love
In harmony with the rhythm of Grace
Sung from my throne above.

Prayer

Heavenly Father

All creation sings a song of praise and worship to Christ our Lord and Savior. Jesus Himself said that if they refuse to worship Him even the stones would cry out. I don't want the rocks and stones singing in my place Father. I sing and worship and dance at Your feet Jesus because You are worthy. When life doesn't seem to be going the way we plan it's good to shift gears and just sing to You Jesus. Just sing. Please help us all carry a melody of Grace in our hearts all day long so that we can sing and worship You throughout our day. When the day is too hard and our burden too heavy, sing with us and uplift our spirit to carry us through. Fill us with joy and hope as we dance to Your rhythm of Grace.

In Jesus name
Amen

MASTER OF THE WAVES

*~ Thank You Jesus for knowing what storms
lie ahead and preparing us beforehand*

You're not set aside nor forgotten
You're being prepared for a coming season
You're being seasoned and tempered for a purpose
Your purpose is ordained for specific time and reason

All things have to be done in the order
That the Spirit has prepared for you
Even if it doesn't make sense
Even if it's not the logical thing to do

You have to trust that your heart knows best
Trust that He who holds Your heart will guide
Believe that no matter what you see or hear
He's always right there with you by your side

He died on the Cross to purchase that right
He rose from the Grave to claim that special place
You're justified and made Righteous by Him alone
Now there's no anger or judgement upon His face

You're being seasoned for what lies ahead
Prepared for things which You cannot see
You don't know what is waiting for you
It's your job to be patient and just believe

Believe that His love for You has made a way
Have Faith that His vision for Your life can never fail
He is the very breath inside Your lungs
And His breath can hold back the strongest gale

The storm is coming one day up ahead
This time of seasoning is necessary to keep you grounded
Because on the Rock of Jesus He's building Your house
His love is the only sure thing on which to be founded

The Cross secured His place inside Your heart
He lives inside but we also live inside Him
His Spirit guides ever towards His voice
A beautiful and enchanting melodic hymn

Once your ears hear that special tone
The wondrous song of Grace our Savior sings
We close our eyes so that every fiber of our being
Receives the love and Grace His voice brings

You've not been forgotten during the storm
You're anchored in safe harbor for what lies ahead
Don't focus on moving forward just yet
Let the calm waters bring you peace instead

The storm is coming and because of this time
You'll be ready to face the winds and turbulent seas
Because the Master of the wind and waves goes with You
The storm knows the voice of the Prince of Peace

Prayer

Father,

Thank You for always preparing us for what lies ahead. There is no way we can know the struggles we will have to face in the next season of our lives but You do Lord. So You go about the process of molding us and working into our hearts those things we'll need so that we can stand victorious in the days ahead. In the natural we cannot see things moving and it seems our goals and dreams have just gone by the wayside. Please help us and show us that we're not forgotten and that You have a purpose and plan that's already been set in motion in our lives and that since You began the work You will see it through to completion. Help us trust in Your timing and in Your plans for our lives and help us submit and hand over our dreams and goals into Your hands. Trusting that what is meant for us will remain and what isn't will be replaced by something better that You already had in store and being readied for our lives. Help us hold strong in the waiting.

In Jesus name
Amen

TRUTH INSIDE

*~With lies and secrets all around us, thank You
Jesus for being Truth we can count on*

His strength in me is perfected
When my strength is gone
When my feet fail me
He gives me wings to carry on

His love for me perfected
This life fraught with pain
His Hope is my anchor
His Grace is my chain

When I don't have the will
To even my open eyes
He gives me eyes of faith
Vision to see thru the disguise

Veils and masks all around
Secrets and lies that divide
We get caught trying to uncover
The truth the world tries to hide

But Truth is actually a person
Beautifully mingled with Grace
His love for me is unchanging
My true home is His Secret Place

Truth cannot be found
In this world infected with sin
Real Truth lives inside us
It bursts forth from within

Grace and Truth took up residence
My heart His permanent address
He Himself came down for me
On the Cross He gave me His very best

Now when the lies of the world
Chokes my heart steals my air
I close my eyes to see Truth inside
Love and Grace chases away despair

The Truth is He decided He'll just love me
In ways i cannot even describe
Sometimes its best to be still
Trust in His love and just abide

Prayer

Father

Sometimes no matter what direction we turn our eyes, all we see are secrets and lies. We look into the eyes of our friends and loved ones and into our own eyes in the mirror and we see that we're all wearing masks to hide away and shelter us from all the deception around us. The lies choke us and steal life away. This world is full of lies from the father of lies and it tears us up on the inside. Keeps us apart. Keeps us on edge afraid to let down our walls, afraid to take off our masks to let anyone see and experience the real us. The only real truth in this life is the truth of who You are Jesus because You came brining Grace and Truth to a world lost in sin. So we look inside, examine ourselves and you teach us to see ourselves through your eyes full of Grace and Truth. Truth is within us because the Spirit of Truth is here to teach us in all things and You came to bring us Grace and Truth to this world full of lies. Help us keep focused on the truth inside us. . . . You. . . . The truth that You loved us so much You went to the Cross and died for us so to redeem us and save us from ourselves. Thank You for Your sacrifice and for making a way to bring us home to heaven with You.

In Jesus name
Amen

TO TRUST IN CHRIST ALONE

~ Thank You Jesus for the peace we have in
Your finished work at the Cross

What does it mean
To trust in Christ alone
Its to rest in His finished work
I have no righteousness of my own

To trust that His love extends
Across all matter time and space
And reaches me in my life today
Filling my heart with love and Grace

Its trusting that on the Cross
Somehow my Lord saw me
He willingly accepted my punishment
Became my ransom and chose to bleed

I am the thief on the cross
I was sentenced to death for my sin
But Jesus overruled my verdict
Now my victory is a gift from Him

Im seated with Christ in heavenly places
When He calls me home I'll receive my crown
I hold my head high in the victory
He won for me now Grace abounds

I trust He made for me a way
To walk on water over stormy seas
And with His Spirit He placed inside me
We wage war hands folded on bended knees

Love is the Way that Christ chose
Grace and Truth the weapons He wields
Abundant Life is found in Him alone
His Grace carries us to harvest fields

One day when my feet lift off the ground
Indescribable beauty will my eyes behold
The Cross is my anchor of hope
Before His throne I can now be bold

To trust in Christ alone is Life
To trust in Christ alone is Truth
To trust in Christ alone is the Way
The empty tomb is our proof

In our weakness is where we find His strength
Through tidal waves of Love and Grace
When you put your trust in Christ alone
You'll surely see Fathers proud smiling face

Prayer

Heavenly Father,

It is good for us to trust in Christ alone because we have no righteousness of our own; no holiness of our own; no good work we ever do is good enough to earn us a way back to Your arms. We need Christ. We need Him not just for salvation, which is a beautiful miraculous gift in and of itself, but we need Him in our daily walk. Our daily struggles become more meaningful and more fulfilling when we walk with HIm right beside us as our Best Friend. Jesus You give us purpose. You give this life meaning. You make this life worth living. Thank you for giving us all of Yourself at the Cross so that we know today that we have access to ALL of YOU in ALL of the areas of our lives and hearts.

In Jesus name
Amen

SEALED WITH A KISS

~Jesus thank You for being so near it's as if I get to kiss your cheek every time I say the words "in Jesus name."

Every promise issued from God
That we read about in His Word
Every blessing issued from His lips
Sanctified in the Name we've heard

We boldly go before our Father
Lay our crowns down at His feet
Trusting by His Love and Grace
Our every need He will meet

Father hears every word we whisper
He hears every tear we've cried
Every pain and hurt we endure
He's right here with us by our side

Our Lord is sitting on His throne
We offer our prayers up to Him
When we say "in Jesus name"
It seals our prayer with a kiss amen

At Calvary the promise is seen
Written in Blood His Word fulfilled
The tomb was Father's Kiss to show
That in Jesus every promise sealed

So now when we pray to our King
We seal each one when we say
"in Jesus name" so it's as if
We kissed His cheek that day

No need to shout just whisper
Your prayers in Jesus ear
Yet each word carries like thunder
For all creation far and near

"In Jesus name" is a gentle kiss
You place upon Lord Jesus cheek
"In His name" your words carry authority
Because it's His heart you seek

Prayer

Heavenly Father,

Thank You for the beautiful gift of Your Son and for loving us and hearing every prayer that falls from our lips. Thank You for the intimate way You revealed Your love for us by offering up Your only Son for us up on the Cross to die to save us. Thank You for breaking down the walls in our own hearts so that we can see the glory of Christ's work at the Cross and at the tomb. As Christ is so are we now in this life. Christ is seated at Your right hand, so near to You that He can just whisper to You Father and You hear Him. That's how near we are to You, all we need to do is whisper softly into Christ's ear and You are right there Abba and we have Your full attention. We need only whisper an intimate prayer into Your ear and You whisper to our hearts Your reply. When we whisper the words "in Jesus name" it's as if we as sealing the prayer at the end with a little kiss on Your cheek from son to Father. A prayer sealed with a kiss to thank You Abba for Your beautiful Son's sacrifice. You honor Your Son by bathing Him in all glory and power and dominion and You give us the precious gift, the beautiful right to pray in Your Son's name and we are so loved by You Father that You answer us as if He HImself prayed. In Jesus name **Kiss on the cheek. Father thank You for being so very close to us and thank You for the beautiful gift of Your only Son.

In Jesus name [kiss]
Amen

OUR PERFECT FRIEND

~ Thank You Jesus for being a friend closer than a brother.

When we are children
We hear about our Father's love
How He's always watching over
Looking down on us from above

We learn He will always love us
No matter what happens in this life
He'll be with us every step we take
In this world that's filled with strife

As we grow up we encounter
Turmoil along the way
We get distracted hurt and broken
Focused on the pain we feel today

We forget that in our Lord
We have the perfect friend
We forget about His promise
He walks with us to the end

His love for us is perfect
He never fails nor leaves our side
And though we make mistakes
From His gaze no need to hide

Nothing could ever compare
With the love He feels for us
We must look with eyes of faith
Believe in our heart in Him we trust

When you fix your eyes upon the Cross
And see the blood dripping from each nail
Believe He's made a way for you
And that His love for you cannot fail

The hurts and pains slowly drift away
Each one consumed by Grace
You'll find He's never left your side
Forever Love and Mercy upon His Face.

Prayer

Heavenly Father,

Your Son Jesus is our Lord, King, Redeemer, Salvation, Savior, our Hope, our help in times of danger, our Faithful and True Witness. . . . But of all the beautiful titles Your Word gives to Him, for He is worthy, the most beautiful is our Friend Who is Closer than a Brother. It tells us that Yes he is our God. . . . But He isn't on some far away throne unreachable to us. So lofty and high not even our prayers could reach His ears. . . no Jesus is our Best Friend and is always right here with us by our side. Walking this lift fraught with hurts and pains right here with us, His love for us never waivers and the magnitude of our sins don't scare Him away because He's already died for them and paid the cost for each and every single one long ago on a lonely hill. He's my Friend Papa. Thank You Jesus for being so much more than we can ever comprehend and even much much more than that. Thank You for the intimate and personal way You have chosen to participate in our lives with us.

In Jesus name
Amen